geography of the forehead

Other Poetry Books by Ron Koertge

The Father Poems
12 Photographs of Yellowstone
Life on the Edge of the Continent
High School Dirty Poems
Making Love to Roget's Wife

geography

of the

forehead

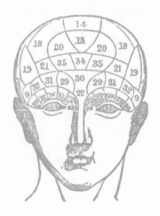

RON
KOERTGE

The University of Arkansas Press
Fayetteville
2000

Designed by Liz Lester

Library of Congress Cataloging-in-Publication Data

Koertge, Ronald.
        Geography of the forehead / Ron Koertge.
            p.   cm.
        ISBN 1-55728-611-6 (pbk. : alk. paper)
        I. Title.
    PS3561.O347 G46 2000
    811'.54—dc21   00-010165

For my wife, Bianca,
who has sat through 10,000 poetry readings

ACKNOWLEDGMENTS

Alaska Quarterly Review: "Werewolf, 1999," "Waiting for My Wife"

Another Chicago Magazine: "Expulsion from the Isle of Forgetfulness."

Apallachee Quarterly: "Matinee"

Columbia Poetry Review: "Miss American Poetry"

Cider Press Review: "Fault," "The Doctor Sighs"

Fourteen Hills: "The Seasons"

Herman Review: "Dear Superman"

Laurel Review: "Noah Webster," "Sunday School," "Truth Serum," "Word Origins," *"Gorilla at Large,"* "Geography of the Forehead," "Monster Week"

Poems & Plays: "American Movie Classics," "Domestic Allegory," "Idolatry"

Rio Grande Review: "Quicksand," "Truth & Beauty"

Plum Review: "'Even Ornaments of Speech Are Forms of Deceit.,'" "Nightclubs"

Solo: "Old & Neglected," "Why I Believe in God," "1989," "Dear Dracula"

"1989" was included in *Best American Poetry, 1999*

Thanks once again to the National Endowment for the Arts (1991) and the California Arts Council (1993). I still find these awards encouraging.

CONTENTS

I

II

███

Miss American Poetry

At the contest in Atlantic City, my poems
are surprised when a sestina isn't a nap
after lunch. And they're amazed that
blank verse is about anything at all.

Things even get sticky at the mixer. A tall
judge leers. "So you're free verse. I've heard
about you." He leans in. "I have a huge
thesaurus. Up in my room."

On the big day, my poems know World Peace
is the answer to every question, but in the talent
portion, it's hard to see their wisps of irony even
from the good seats. Clutching the Congeniality
Certificate, they fly home.

Meanwhile the local magazines are in the town
square—smoking, revving their engines,
combing their considerable hair.

Dear Dracula

This diet of yours is so cool. Just a few pints a day
and I'm like really thin. My old boyfriends are totally
after me now, but no way! All they ever wanted was
you-know-what and make it quick. God, the way you
licked my wrist! You took hours.

I told my mom those holes in my neck were a fad,
like nose rings. She bought it! And don't worry
about Dad. He's so checked out, the walking
dead if you know what I mean.

I can't wait for tonight, Count D. I love it
when you do that thing with your cape!
And then we have to chat. My folks are after
me to go to city college. But now I couldn't
stay awake in class, anyway, and if I'm going
to live forever, what's the hurry, right?

I've been thinking, though. I want to be special,
not just another long, white neck. Let's face it. You're
like 9000 years older than me. You've really been
around. So maybe when we fly back to your castle
in Pennsylvania, I should at least go to night school.

We'll talk, okay? Right now I have to put the crucifix
away, throw a towel over the mirror, then get into
my jammies. Oh, and brush my teeth which, I have
to tell you, seems to take a little longer all the time.

Moving

Brides wave good-bye in their swany
camouflage. Boy Scouts set out
for University of the Weed. Sheep
abandon their meadows to aid
the sleepless. Ghosts leave the home
of the body, and snow its cozy cloud.
Even comets pack their fiery bags
and head out around the sun.

But the cat weaves among boxes,
revolves in the tall grass of memory,
and lies down with a sigh—at home
anywhere.

Redondo

Beneath my feet the pier shifts
and drools. Above, some gulls carve
out the sturdy air as surfers arrange
themselves like quarter notes across
a distant wave.

It is a relief to stop staring at girls,
to quiet the heart's thick strokes
and calmly pass the man with a truant
officer's scowl, a boy writing a post card
(that small hymn), and then the great
great-grandchildren of Lady Macbeth
washing their hands again and again
at the edge of the unraveling world.

What a place to have God rear His
amazing head. Yet here I am, all
the clutter inside made in Your image.
The ocean is forever changing its clothes
to be more beautiful for You. There
is the horizon which You have drawn
with a golden rule and outlined, too,
a tiny ship and curl of smoke to make
the scene complete.

Gorilla at Large

My mother isn't feeling well, so I tell her
I'll come over and we'll just watch TV.
What's on is *Gorilla at Large,* starring Ann
Bancroft and Raymond Burr. Since the operation
she's not interested in much, but this movie
has her sitting up in bed.

There's a cute guy with biceps, some blackmail,
and a murder. Ann flounces around in her skimpy
circus costume, Raymond gets jealous, the gorilla
leers and shakes the bars of his cage.

Mom is particularly tender-hearted these days.
She's been calling everyone whose feelings
she might have hurt. She's asked bitter
enemies to come to the hospital.

So she cries when the gorilla scrambles
to the top of the roller coaster and is shot.
But she hasn't got one kind word for
Ann Bancroft as she's led away to jail.

She gropes for the spot on her night table
where the cigarettes used to be, then gets
out of bed and shambles toward the bathroom.

"There was a woman like that set her cap
for your father once. I showed her a thing
or two."

Ah, there's the mother I loved and feared.
Not the one with her hands folded on
the pink quilted bed jacket. But this one—
drinking straight from the tap, scratching
her behind, leering at me with huge,
yellow, affectionate teeth.

Q and A

What exactly is a thesaurus?

> A thesaurus is like a thousand family
> reunions, all in the same hotel, but each
> one in a separate ballroom. A dictionary,
> on the other hand, is like the Army where
> everyone lines up for roll call.

Do words have feelings?

> Absolutely. One picture can burden a
> thousand words with low self-esteem.

How can I have a large vocabulary?

> Exercise. Start with *air, leaf, inch.* Then
> increase slowly. Be patient and careful.
> The first time you try *incarnadine,*
> have someone spot you.

Do words die?

> Of course. I remember the funeral
> of *a go-go.* She looked completely natural
> in her black boots, miniskirt, and fringed
> blouse.

How can I remember the parts of speech?

> Picture a fancy restaurant: An adjective
> lights the cigarette of a noun. Two adverbs
> accompany a verb to the rest room. An
> article holds the door; a preposition hands
> the verb a warm hand towel.

I Meet My Father on the Stairs

and he's tiny. Say, this is fun
pushing him around, making
him chew 30 times. It's great

to see him fry as I bellow
at his wife and he can't
do anything. Then I feel

a little sorry for him.
He's so grateful for a pat
on the head that he cries

and pees in the heavy
canvas pants he wears
to work on the night shift.

Word Origins

Sonnet comes from the Old Provençal
for *poem,* but that doesn't help much.
So we must walk back in time past
Late Greek glancing at his sundial
and Low German swearing at a
bratwurst until we come to Latin,
so young it is still wearing the collar
of its jacket up.

And there we find sound + et = *sonus:*
A little sound, the kind the first poet
might make as he stared in frustration
at the earth, drawing his rake through
the smooth dirt, gazing at the fourteen
empty lines, thinking of his beloved,
what he would say to her, how he would
say it if only he could find a way.

Wolf

When I saw tattered pelts strung
along barbed wire and when I heard
ranchers tally and grin, I wondered

if those were the wolves Mother
crooned about at bedtime, the ones
who coughed in Russian, walked on
hind legs, and knew boys from girls.

They chased sleighs across frozen lakes,
blew on houses of wood and straw,
slipped into granny's feather bed,
and lay there panting

so that my parents, who knew the world
was cold and dangerous, could close
the tattered book, pull the comforter tight
and kiss me harder than they meant to.

"Even Ornaments of Speech Are Forms of Deceit."

History of the Royal Society

It's 1667. Reason is everywhere, saving
for the future, ordering a small glass of wine.
Cause, arm in arm with Effect, strolls by
in sturdy shoes.

Of course, there are those who venture
out under cover of darkness to buy a bag
of metaphors or even some personification
from Italy, primo and uncut.

But for the most part, poets like Roderigo
stroll the boulevards in their normal hats.
When he thinks of his beloved, he opens
his notebook with a flourish.

"Your lips," he writes, "are like
lips."

Signs & Miracles

"If You exist," I said, "send me
a pony."

Immediately Jesus appeared
in my bedroom.

I got off my knees. "You heard
my prayer!"

He quoted Himself: "Except ye
see signs and miracles, you will
not believe."

"Be reasonable, Jesus. It's hard
to just take Your word for it."

"But I'm here. In your bedroom.
Isn't that enough?"

"So is the pony outside?"

"And a Few of Your Thoughts on Writing, Please"

I used to think that to write poetry
I needed absolute silence, so I could hear
the muse in her bare feet.

I imagined special pens, ink the color
of Shelly's eyes, and paper made only
from trees that had died in a hospice,
their pulp then pressed into quartos
by celibate vegetarians.

Certainly I needed a thesaurus as heavy
as Roget's daughter, gold-leafed encyclopedia
filling hand-polished bookshelves, and perhaps
something cashmere for the higher altitudes
of Art.

Now I seem to need nothing but a room
and a cat. Outside, the gardener writes
his long, green sentences. In here, JoJo
steps through the window and fixes me
with his voluptuous eyes.

I pick up the stub of a pencil and go to work.

Geography of the Forehead

Everyone thinks the brain is so complicated,
but let's look at the facts. The frontal lobe,
for example, is located in the front! And
the temporal lobe is where the clock is.
What could be simpler?

The hippocampal fissure is where big, dumb
thoughts camp, while at the Fissure of Rolando
dark-skinned men with one gold earring lie
around the fire and play guitars.

The superior frontal convolution is where
a lot of really nice houses are set back off
a twisty road, while the inferior frontal
convolution is a kind of trailer park, regularly
leveled by brainstorms.

The area of Broca is pretty much off limits.
And if you know Broca, you know why.

American Movie Classics

As I watch the library clerk pluck books from the night-
drop and trundle them toward the big door, I can't help
but think of Richard Egan. In nearly every movie, he
escapes from prison in a cart just like that.

Free at last, he's dying to prove he's been blackmailed,
but before that he wants to see his fiancée. She lives
on the first floor of a rooming house. Her door is open.
The bed is made. She's reading a book.

"Sweetheart," she cries, "I was just thinking about you!"
He smiles like Richard Egan. "I need to see Mr. Big, baby.
He can clear things with the cops. Get ready."

Richard Egan polishes his uppercut for some pretty
boy and maybe that broad in the silver shoes, too,
as his girl puts her good blouse and scarf in a battered suitcase.

She looks around the room, then murmurs, "Oh, that book
I borrowed. On the way out of town, can we drop by
the library?"

That grin of his. That white shirt with the top buttons
torn off in a fight. Those big hands in her intellectual hair.

Gretel

said she didn't know anything about ovens,
so the witch crawled in to show her
and Bam! went the big door.

Then she strolled out to the shed where
her brother was fattening, knocked down
a wall, and lifted him high in the air.

Not long after the adventure in the forest
Gretel married so she could live happily.
Her husband was soft like Hansel. Her
husband liked to eat.

Ever after was the size of a kitchen.
Gretel remembered when times were better.
She'd laughed out loud when the witch
popped like a weenie.

"Gretel! Stop fooling around and fix
my dinner."

"There's something wrong with this oven,"
she says, her eyes bright as treasure.
"Can you come here a minute?"

The Arrival

More than one Chinese poem begins with spring
coming to the women's quarters, and this movie
is like that:

a boardinghouse in Hollywood, hopeful gals
on the porch, mock orange scenting the air.

A gangly cut-up strums her ukulele.
Then someone says, "Hey, kids, let's head south
of the border for some real fun."

Bongos and maracas appear and a brassy
blonde named Mabel starts a conga line.

I know this doesn't seem much like a Chinese
poem yet, but just wait. Joan Crawford
is about to step out of a producer's roadster

and stand there like the emperor's horse
waiting for concubines to throw their hair
across the path.

Matinee

At first I think the sound of sloshing water
comes from the feature next door in Mann's
cozy triplex, but then, preceded by a wedge
of light, all these dead parents file in.

Immediately I ask them a lot of questions
about my version of heaven and if a love
as clumsy as mine is okay, too.

But one says, "Shhh" and hands me a frozen
treat. "It's called God's Breath." So I'm happy
to sit there and lick until, abruptly, the dead
parents get up and begin kissing some of us

good-bye. And as much as I want to lift my
light-bandaged face toward their immaterial
lips, I also want to know why Margo clutches
her torn red blouse as Rex leaps from his Volvo.

That evening I tell my wife. "Really?" she says
basting the fish. "Really?" she says pouring
more wine. "Well, what did God's Breath taste
like?" she asks giving me more salad than I
could possibly eat.

The Doctor Sighs

as he removes the otoscope.
"It's not just the hammer,
anvil, and stirrup," he says.
"It's the blacksmith, too.
And the dry goods store
with the weaselly clerk,
not to mention the saloon
rife with cowboys and
a prostitute with humble
cleavage. And I'm afraid
it's also the calibrated hearts
in that freezing ten-room
hotel, the mayor's daughter
weeping into well water,
the moon spreading its
anxious light over everything.

In short, Ronald, I'm not
surprised you called
for an appointment today."

Dear Superman

I know you think that things
will always be the same: I'll rinse
out your tights, kiss you good-bye
at the window, and every few weeks
get kidnapped by some stellar goons.

But I'm not getting any younger,
and you're not getting any older.
Pretty soon I'll be too frail
to take aloft, and with all those
nick-of-time rescues, you're bound
to pick up somebody more tender
and just as ga-ga as I used to be.
I'd hate her for being 17 and you
for being . . . what, 700?

I can see your sweet face as you read
this, and I know you'd like to siphon
off some strength for me, even if it
meant you could only leap small buildings
at a single bound. But you can't,
and, anyway, would I want to
just stand there while everything
else rushed past?

Take care of yourself and of the world
which is your own true love. One day
soon, as you patrol the curved earth,
that'll be me down there tucked in
for good, being what you'll never be
but still

    Your friend,
    Lois Lane

On My Honor

I knew boys who could make fire
from snow, boys who knew how to suck
poison and save the world.

But the thighs of the Scoutmaster made me
sick. And my baby-sitter would let me
watch her bathe if I promised not to tell.

My good deed was helping her out of the tub,
holding her plush hand aloft. Once I fainted
and hit my head. When I came to, she was

still naked, crouched over me. I could taste
the blood and the ache and began right then
to work toward a merit badge in Desire.

Last Saturday Night

My students were so flattered I came to
the party that they installed me in a soft
chair, and everybody filed by like I was
a king. An old king.

They don't think it will happen to them.
I heard Teresa say that she will kill
herself first, leaving scores of broken-
hearted lovers to fall on their swords
or swallow pills.

Maybe. The boyfriend she has now is
sweet but so dense he is more likely to
swallow his sword. Or fall on some pills.

By 10:00 the king is sleepy, so they
tell me to watch my step and drive
carefully. Of course, they're thinking
if I do make it home, soon there'll
be a tall, cloaked figure at the door.

And my only hope is to croak, "Who died
by water, Shelley or Keats?" Then as he
scratches his head with the tip of a scythe
I should run, if I can, for what's left
of my life.

Molly Is Asked

to be in the Christmas pageant. She tells
me this standing in the door of what we
laughingly call my study.

"But I don't want to be Mary," she says.
"I want to be the guy."

That makes me look up from my bills.
"Joseph?"

"The innkeeper. I want to slam the door
in Joseph's face."

She's eight. I wonder if we'll look back
on this next year and laugh. Or will she
want to be Herod and we'll have to take
her little brother and flee.

Old & Neglected

Of course nobody ever calls them
that because they were willing
extras in the movie, sidekicks
for the handsome and charismatic,
donkey, ox, and dromedary
in the crèche of poetry.

Willing to the end, they stand
on the platform waving good-bye
to the new & selected, passing
lunches through the window,
even playing in the band, sweating
in the scratchy uniforms.

And when that streamliner
has pulled away, their train chugs
up. Next stop Obscurity, where
it's always June, couples must walk
hand in hand toward a twenty-four-
hour sunset, and everyone lives
beside a warm, slow-moving river
that nevertheless overflows
its banks every Mother's Day.

Domestic Allegory

Jealousy dons a green suit. Beauty
gazes at herself in the mirror. Time
wears a diaper or, all grown up,
a winding sheet.

But today Time wears a skirt.
Time is, in fact, my wife pointing
at the watch I bought for her birthday.

So I have to go now. She is waiting.
And, anyway, this leaf-yellow page
ends a notebook that only yesterday
I thought would last forever.

Quicksand

I loved those jungle movies in the 50s—a good
guy, a bad guy, and a blonde with some vaccine.
But I didn't love the end where the villain fled,
fell into quicksand, and died a slow, gurgling death

because he never changed his shirt, because he'd
found the lost tribe's gold, because he couldn't keep
his eyes off Dr. Kathy's khaki bra.

I didn't like to take a bath, either. I wanted
diamonds from the eyes of idols, too. I wanted
Dr. Kathy drugged in a hammock.

When the matinee was over, the elms of my
hometown were gone, smothered by vines
and fronds. As parrots shrieked, I licked my
cracked lips, hefted the knapsack of rubies
and ran blindly down what used to be

my street even as it started to dissolve and suck
at my boots, the ones I never polished even though
they'd cost my parents a fortune.

Rented Tux

I know that *cummerbund*
is from the Persian for loin band,
but I keep that to myself as Vince
the salesman puts his arms around me.

I wonder how many sloe gin
fizzes this silly shirt has ushered
onto the lap of these enormous pants
where other penises have tolled
mournfully as the reception wore on
or the prom or the end of the year.

When I look in the mirror, I resemble
a man in a drafty hall facing a handful
of bewildered people, a man about to
receive a very small award—something
along the lines of the Golden Pea.

Waiting for My Wife

As the thumbprint of every car
is pressed to the night,

I glance up from the book in my
lap. It's then the pages

begin to turn on their own
in that way books have.

This one wants me to know it
is just as beautiful, just as

cruel. Look how its white
margins hold that story hostage.

Truth & Beauty

Joined at the hip ever since Keats
opened his big yap, Truth & Beauty
decide to go their separate ways.

They stroll down to the Greyhound
station together. One bus has yellow
stripes and a fat driver with a cigar.
The other is dark and facing west
like Whistler's mother.

"Cold out," says Truth. And Beauty,
in a fur-lined hooded jacket with
matching cuffs, replies, "Not really."

Idolatry

I never liked being a Baptist: all those commandments,
a fiery pit, and a heaven that—for all its glories—
doesn't have pari-mutuel wagering.

But my Catholic friends aren't any happier. Ditto
the Lutherans and the Methodists. I know too many
unhappy Jews and Buddhists and one absolutely
miserable Sufi.

So I am thinking of making up my own religion.
First of all, absolutely no crucifixions. I suppose
Jesus could stand in the corner for an hour,
but that's as far as it goes.

And you know those four apocalyptic horses
in the book of Revelations? I'd have ponies—
palomino ponies with names like Muffin and Bev,
Sparky and Bill.

I want about a dozen gods of love, but Kama gets
to be in charge. I'm crazy about his sugarcane bow
strung with honeybees and those five flowered arrows
of desire. For sure, no deities like Shiva the Destroyer.
Maybe Steve, who doesn't signal when he changes lanes.

Of course this is all in the planning stages. The funny
thing is if I have a couple of drinks and blab to some
strangers at a party, they immediately want to join.

I tell them, "Well, gee, it isn't anywhere near finished."

That's when they fall on their knees in front of me.
"It doesn't matter," they cry. "It's so much better
than what we have."

The Red Shirt

My daughter opens a geography book,
points to the deepest green and says,
"There are people there, no one knows
what to call them, and they're all naked.
Can we go?"

It's a pretty picture, isn't it? Liquid
eyes peering out at the explorer Molly,
her name like a red shirt everyone
wants to own.

The Seasons

Summer is from Sanskrit, meaning half-year.
And wonderful as summer is (that flight to the ruins,
those blue rooftops) there is a melancholy about it
as grass leans into the drenched wind and quilters at
Frontier Town begin to bicker and snap at the tourists.

Autumn is the only season with a nickname. But fall
does have overtones of carelessness. Can't you almost
see autumn lying in bed, one leg in a cast, a stern nurse
bullying some cyclamen?

Poor winter with its bare elm and frozen lake, reduced
to zero by night classes in poetry appreciation.

But spring! Just look at the way a polygraph will
gambol across the scroll as a technician hooks
himself up then reads from a yearbook the names
of all the girls he said he loved.

Expulsion from the Isle of Forgetfulness

They like getting out because school sucks,
but the museum sucks, too, and this painting
sucks the most.

"Why?" I ask, ever the textbook educator.
"Well, did she forget her clothes?" asks Karen.
"Is that why the painting's called that?"
"Back then," I begin, "the nude was simply . . ."

Lujuana announces, "My folks forgot me once.
They just went off somewhere for the weekend."
All the baseball hats stir. "That's cold." A few
crumple up their free souvenir postcards.

Other museum-goers begin to give us a wide berth.
"Look, guys," I say. "Take it easy. It's just a . . ."

Michael demands, "And if it's really some
island where people forget, who's even gonna
remember to kick 'em out, huh? Tell me that!"

By now we are alone in the 17th century, glaring
at the polished frame. Then here comes a docent
in her frost-colored shoes.

"Ladies and gentlemen," she says holding onto her
pearls. "Please, try to remember where you are."

Noah Webster

What if God had said to this Noah,
"Prepare a great ship and take on it
all manner of words, two by two."

Enmity and Rancor demand separate
staterooms while Obsequious
and Fawning insist that any old
place is fine with them. Really.

Doubt and Suspicion check their tickets
again while Fastidious tiptoes on
with Meticulous, both carrying cans
of Lysol.

Pomp takes forever to board and Pageantry
isn't much better. Pretentious, left behind,
demands to speak to the person in charge.

Danger and Peril hang from the rigging
and wave good-bye to Risk who is happily
treading water and lighting another
unfiltered cigarette.

The Mr. Death Pageant

As all fifty parade beneath the crepe,
footage from earlier in the week shows
them kidding around with a frayed electrical
cord or soaping the steps to the stage.

In the talent portion, most play the organ
or chant. But Idaho is great with the scythe.
Arizona's icy grip gets raves from the panel.
Nobody beckons from the gloom like Florida.

By midnight there is a new Mr. Death!
As he stalks the footlights and waves,
losers trudge backstage where they're
met by unscrupulous managers who steer
them into X-rated movies or teaching
at the community college.

And sometimes they rise from their mortgaged
beds to stand in an open door and watch the dark
mobile over the crib revolve slowly. How strange
life is, they think. How heartless. How sweet.

World War I

When someone decided to torpedo
passenger ships, the German Prime
Minister resigned. "War," he said,
"is an honorable profession." Then he
turned on one polished heel and left
the whiskey-colored room.

And what happened then, I wonder?
Did he hang around the fatherland
and get in his wife's way? Or
did he do something honorable

like duel so that he had an attractive
scar to caress thoughtfully as
the butler, silver tray aloft, brought
in his paper full of the terrible news.

Monster Week

Monday they kill Frankenstein because he's ugly.
On Tuesday, Wolfman howls at the moon, ruins
a dinner party, and gets a silver bullet for his
trouble. Wednesday the Mummy almost catches
the girl but disintegrates first, and Thursday
there's just this poor robot without any elbows.

By Friday, the only monster left is a Giant Clam
minding his own business. His victims have
to paddle to him. And stick their hand in.
But he gets it anyway, for merely protecting
his creation, a pearl as big as a Brunswick
Strike-Master.

My god, he's barely a monster at all. He's just
irritable, like I am: a pesky word that won't leave
me alone, a title needling me for a first line.

What can I do? One draft after another like
the nacreous laminations of the pearl. Like this
poem that took months to finish.

So, greedy reader, if you know what is good
for you, take your hand off this page before
the book closes over it and you are lost.

The Four Horses of the Apocalypse

We know who rode them, but not who took
care of them. War with his noisy saddlebags?
Not likely. Famine with his one oat? The sooner
Pestilence is out of any stable, the better. While
Death is not the type to take off his sulphurous
cloak and muck out a stall.

So when the big guns dismount at the end
of their apocalyptic day and clatter into
the house, a stable boy with a limp pats each
elegant nose, lifts every hoof to look for stones,
waters them out, washes and curries all the time
saying under his breath the names he knows
them by: Big Boy, Cookie, Suzie Q, Sam.

Paradise Lost

Westlake Memorial Cemetery is bordered
on the north by busy Route 157, but sometimes
a deer steps out of the trees south of plot 272,
nibbles from a mound, then darts away.

Since I only get back here once a year or so, I see
how the toys on the graves of the children change:
Power Rangers replace Ninja Turtles. Red Camaros
are crushed by Widow Maker Monster Trucks.
And the cemetery changes, too, slowly moving west
in the measured tread of progress.

Today, a young poet has slipped his jacket over
the back of my father's grave as if he were saving
someone a seat in assembly. I know he's a poet
because he has a fancy notebook and he wears
his loneliness like a beret.

It says in the Bible that where two or three
poets are gathered together, they tend to form
a circle and nod sympathetically. But this one
is alone, and he scowls at me.

So I stroll to the edge of the bluff where even
the dead will have to stop. A breeze off
the Mississippi turns the page of the evening.
A thousand cicadas sound like Milton
ranting at his daughters.

Why I Believe in God

I'd failed the examination allowing me to bypass the M.A.
    and go straight for a Ph.D., so I was obliged to let
my friends forge ahead reading, if possible, longer and fatter
    books than before while I worked on something
by the Pearl Poet for my thesis.

    My advisor was Mrs. Hamilton, a world-class
medievalist and the most patient lady in the world.
    Every week I'd bring her a few pages of translation.
She would smile and correct everything. With her help,
    I finished.

An orals board consists of three members of the English
    department and someone from another
discipline, usually an assistant professor from chemistry
    who drinks coffee from a beaker. But my guy
was from the German department. He had a scar, for God's
    sake, that might've come from a duel. He
also wanted to begin. Because he had a few questions.

    "Vhat was the root of zis word? Zah root for zhat?
Who in his right mind vould mistake zhat as zis!" I glanced
    at Mrs. Hamilton who looked like she was watching
Thumper get hit by a tank. I took a deep breath and replied
    that I knew I was less prepared in German than
I should have been but German was the very next course
    I planned to take. I then hoped to move
to Germany and become German.

He sneered, but Dr. Rosenblatt, God bless him, asked me
    something easy: What was Eliot's first initial?

Then Mrs. Hamilton wanted to know if Whitman had a beard.
Yes or no would be enough.

I was just getting my sea legs when Dr. Death leaned
forward. "Vhat," he hissed, "is zah function
of zah ghost in *Hamlet*?" Actually he may have been
trying to be nice because it isn't that hard
a question. The ghost is the key that starts the engine
of the play. Without him, Hamlet is just
another pouty prince.

But I froze. I couldn't think of anything.
My teachers stared at me. They leaned forward
encouragingly. "Do you remember the ghost,
Mr. Koertge?" asked Mrs. Hamilton. "Yes, ma'am."
"What was he in the play for?" My mind
was a blank. Less than a blank, a cipher. Less than
a cipher, a black hole. Finally I said,
"Uh, to scare people?"

They almost collapsed. Mrs. Hamilton put her
head in her hands. Dr. Rosenblatt murmured, "Oh, my God."

Then they sent me out of the room. I pictured
myself selling aluminum siding. Or going into the Army.
Or both. Then I heard the arguing begin:
Shakespeare had not been part of my course work. I'd
been blindsided from the beginning by
an arrogant outsider. Mrs. Hamilton said she knew the German's
publisher; all she had to do was pick up
the phone and he would never see another word in print.

They called me back in, said congratulations,
and (all but you-know-who) shook my hand. Mrs. Hamilton
    gave me a hug and said she'd never wanted
a cocktail so badly in her life.

I stepped outside into the Tucson heat. God was sitting on
    the steps in front of Old Main staring at his sandals.
"Ronald!" He waved me over. "I protected you when you
    drove home drunk, I introduced you to Betty Loeffler,
and I just got you through that exam."
    "You know Betty?"
    "You were lonely."
    "Gosh, thanks."
    "You don't believe in Me, but I believe in you. So I'm
interested in what you plan to do next."
    "Not get a Ph.D. I'm a terrible student."
    "You're telling me."
    "I like writing poetry."
God stood up. He had a great smile and, except for those sandals,
    a cool outfit. "Fine. Be a poet. But don't say mean
things about people in your poems. Be generous. Don't be deep
    or obscure. Try and make people laugh." Then, just
before He disappeared, He kissed me. And that is why I am
    standing here tonight.

Skeletons

What a lot of trouble it would save if we
were all bones. No more racial tension,
hair restorer, or diet plans.

We would clatter to the store for milk
(there would be a wide variety of that)
and chat with our neighbors, all those
clacking mandibles giving the Express
Lane a south-of-the-border flavor.

Ah, but I would probably prefer the cashier's
creamy femur, and you might want the box boy
to play the xylophone of your vertebrae.

Nothing, not even Halloween, would console
us from the certain knowledge that we are,
even stripped to the barest necessities,
still human.

The Cisco Kid

I'm sitting on this fine white horse.
The schoolteacher takes off her spectacles
and sighs. The citizens mill around.
Now that they're safe, they want me gone.
But I can't ride on without Pancho,
who's behind that haystack with the chubby girl.

I'm a goddamned icon, so before the fire
goes out tonight, he'll have to tell me
about her hair, her breasts, her face
lit with human love.

The Huntington Library

For seven dollars, I get Henry himself
standing in his painted shoes beside
a perfect hound. And then behind
a velvet rope, his writing desk waiting
for still another letter to a lazy king.
And then the glittering bed, its canopy
like sacred smoke. And then and then . . .

I just want to go home where a cat
sleeps on the sports page, a frazzled
toothbrush leans in its milky glass.
Probably my wife has gone back to bed
and I could join her there, leaving
in a pile by the door the pants I wore
yesterday, too.

55

is outside the door. For now, I am opening
gifts. Here is *Best Loved Poems*. I hold it up
to my neck like a tie and everyone laughs.

Then I read aloud. All the poems are about
Jesus and dogs. I start a little riff about how
few pets there are in the Bible.

Moses didn't have one. It's hard to picture
Herod with a kitten or Judas holding a parakeet
on his not-quite-clean finger.

My friends are drunk enough, so they laugh
then kiss me good-bye like people leaving
a sinking ship—women and children first.

Alone, I clean up a little. 55 has slipped in,
but we aren't on speaking terms yet. Still,
when I put the cake on the table and pick

at my name, it comes and looks over my shoulder.
I can feel the warmth from its little pot belly.
Its breath is sweeter than I thought it would be.

Ironing

There is just something about it—
standing here in nothing but my gunbelt—
that I like.

Girlfriends of the Magi

When I feel him coming, I start saving
water for a bath. I borrow scarves
and jewels. I eat nothing but grapes
for days because he likes me thin.

That night I kiss his tired thighs,
comb out his beard. I want to play
a game where home is the mole beside
my breast and then he travels south.

But this new place is different, he says,
and fumbles for a map and shows me
but his finger never leaves the narrow path.

I've been burning like a lamp turned low
for months. Now he says he wants to talk.
Two tents away is someone else who knows
the stars. She says a terrible time is coming.

Is this the beginning of that?

Truth Serum

Someone is tied to a bed or a chair.
A doctor—usually alcoholic, always
needing a shave—administers the dose
from a huge syringe.

Gritting his teeth and sweating bullets,
the G.I. or private investigator struggles
not to reveal the combination to the safe,
the number of troops bivouacked by
the river, or the spy's code name.

Fine. But what I want to know is, why doesn't
the person start telling the rest of the truth:
"Gee, it's hot in here! These ropes aren't
tight enough to get me excited. Who picked
the wallpaper for this room? You couldn't pay
me to drive a Chevy. When it comes to chairs,
stackability is more important then style. If I
don't go to the bathroom right after breakfast,
my whole day is ruined!"

Half an hour of that and even the sadistic
commandant with the monocle would cry,
"Stop, for God's sake. Have mercy. I'll
tell you anything, if you'll just stop."

Foolish Earthlings

That's what they call us, those icky guys
from somewhere out there with their syrupy
heads or tin lips. And right after we've
welcomed them with open arms and let
them take our homecoming queen and her
first runner-up on a tour of the saucer's
medical facilities.

No wonder the dorky scientist is ticked off.
No wonder he and the trim first lieutenant
work so hard to find a chink in the DNA.
And naturally they succeed and just in time.
So the fiends from Cygnus lose again.

Here's some advice for spacemen. Take it
easy with the scorn. Learn a couple of jokes,
buy a round when it's your turn, keep your
eyes (all your eyes, pal) off our daughters.
Say, "We come in peace." Say it a lot.
We're suckers for that.

Flaubert in Egypt

Before he left for Cairo, Flaubert arranged his studio
to look as if he would be back in the morning: pen
beside notebook, uncapped inkwell, dressing gown
thrown over a chair. He felt he might turn around
at any moment and rush home. "I could give my
mother this tremendous joy." He could also
immediately go back to work.

But on what? Epileptic attacks had excused him
from law school, so he could do what he liked—
live at home and write. But the writing didn't go
well. And his mother hovered. And he'd just broken
off his affair, mostly epistolary, with Louise Colet.
Why not go. Because, "The journey is too long, too
distant. What madness!" Finally managing to tear
himself away, his mother screamed when he closed
the door behind him. He sent her four letters
from Paris, one from Lyon, and two from Marseilles
even before he sailed.

He was twenty-eight years old. There are no pictures
of him, but he was said to be tall, handsome, and vigorous.
In one of his first letters from Cairo, he wrote that his
mouth was so sensuous women regretted that it was
hidden under a moustache. Of course, he wasn't telling
Mama things like that. To her—"How peaceful are the
depths we feel our minds explore." To his friend Louis
Bouilhet, however—"Good brothels no longer exist in
Cairo." And that was unfortunate because "One learns
so many things in brothels, one feels such sadness, and

dreams so longingly of love!" So he and his companion
Maxime du Camp sailed up the Nile, marveled at Egypt's
black soil, read at Memphis where fleas on the pages
looked like agitated punctuation, and listened to songs
that made them restless: "O, God, sweet it is to suck
nectar from her mouth."

He'd heard the story of Madame Delamare, a spoiled
young woman married to a medical officer. She made
her servants address her as "Your Prettiness," spent
obsessively, took lovers, ruined her life and her
husband's. But in Egypt, he wrote only in a journal,
because "travel enlivens one's style."

Anyway, he was busy seeing snake charmers
and dervishes, reading Homer, shooting doves,
confiding to a friend, "Haven't I everything
enviable in the world? Independence, the
freedom of my fancy, two hundred trimmed pens,
and the art of using them."

But he wasn't using them. He was years away
from sixteen hour days of composition and revision.
How could he even guess that he would vomit three
times writing Emma's death scene or that one day
he would crow, "Madame Bovary, c'est moi!"

Halfway through the trip he writes to his mother
yet again, argues with DuCamp, then hires a prostitute
who demands to be paid in advance. He makes vigorous
love to her, holding her necklace between his teeth
and staining the divan, though later he would confide

that in the morning, of course, she would think of him no more than any of the others.

What a relief to return to France, to his mother that old darling, to his beloved studio and those faithful objects—pen and paper, the tea cup, the candle waiting to shed its finite, undemanding light.

Fault

In the airport bar, I tell my mother not to worry.
No one ever tripped and fell into the San Andreas
Fault. But as she dabs at her dry eyes, I remember
those old movies where the earth does open.

There's always one blonde entomologist, four
deceitful explorers, and a pilot who's good-looking
but not smart enough to take off his leather jacket
in the jungle.

Still, he and Dr. Cutie Bug are the only ones
who survive the spectacular quake because
they spent their time making plans to go back
to the Mid-West and live near his parents

while the others wanted to steal the gold and ivory
then move to Los Angeles where they would rarely
call their mothers and almost never fly home
and when they did for only a few days at a time.

Sinatra

Every drunk in the world
comes to his last concert.

Frank sings all the old songs,
the great ones, as the swizzle
sticks pile up.

They're so happy they start
to bawl. And then, get this,

he comes down off that stage,
takes off his toupee and wipes
their faces with it!

What a fuckin' guy.

Werewolf, 1999

It used to be when one of my ancestors
looked up at the full moon, he soon found
himself snarling and tearing at someone's
brocade, only to wake the next morning
in another ruined suit.

But over the decades, a curse thins,
blood cools. Now the countess loves
moonlight. She wears loose trousers,
and I fetch a stick. We roughhouse
in front of the fire. When she bathes,
I open the door with my smart muzzle
and listen to her sing.

Lying at her feet as she eats from a simple
bowl, I dread the next morning: problems
with the gamekeeper, servants who steal,
a ball we have to attend, the horrible soup
that begins an endless banquet with us
at either end of a Regency table dressed
to kill and longing for a full moon.

Sunday School

We were hard to handle, even at nine. We didn't
want to bring in the stupid sheaves or turn
the other cheek. We liked taking God's name
in vain. We coveted everything, especially
the Technicolor

slides those Lutherans had while we stared
at a dumb flannel-graph: Jesus and Paul
and some sheep which, Mr. Bowman said,
is what we were while He was our shepherd.

God, I hated that. So when he was called out
of the room, I dashed up, made Jesus lie
on top of Paul and had a sheep kiss them both
on the mouth.

We squirmed in our seats, boiling with anticipation.
When Mr. Bowman came back, he glanced at
the flannel-graph and, we couldn't believe it,
he smiled.

I'd never thought twice about him before that. He
was just a grown-up to make fun of. But I suddenly
saw into him, the way I saw into my feet through
the fluoroscope at the Buster Brown shoe store.

And I loved him, the way the Bible told me to.

Against "Untitled"

Let's say poems live in a town all their own.
Free verse opens a massage parlor, haiku
run the macrobiotic restaurant, doggerel
howls when a fire engine goes by, sonnets
gaze up at shuttered windows, a sestina
runs the copy shop.

Your poem lives there, too, and crossing Blue
Guitar St., is hit by a bus. Its wallet says
"Untitled," so it's sent to the morgue with
Jonathan Doe dangling from one iambic foot.

Not a pretty picture, is it. And how about your
new poems, all untitled, all standing in the street
red-faced and squalling as everyone else is
called in to dinner.

"What Are Writers Really Like?"

question from the audience

Some are like the horse
who is comfortable
in a harness of prose.

Others resemble the elephant
who can carry giant lies
and not stumble.

But most of us are like dogs:
mysterious pads
roving across bond,

a long red tongue
falling all over
an immaculate page.

Smoke

The summer I was sixteen I worked second
shift. "Lumber's here," said the foreman.
"I want it there."

I held up my end, drank two gallons of water,
didn't fold like a Texaco map. On the way
home I stopped at Fairmount Park.

It was such a dinky track that anybody tall
enough to push his dollar through the mouse
hole in the Plexiglas could get in.

I eyed the horses with the biggest odds.
I thought a hundred dollars would change
everything.

"Who do you like?" asked a guy with duct
tape on his boots. I said, "Fancy Hooves."
We watched her win. He shook out two
Camels. "Know what a parlay is?"

When I walked in the house, my dad took
one look at me and said, "Get him an ashtray."
Mom took her look and got it.

The Two-Poem Warning

We all do it. We look up from the podium,
glance at our watches, flip through the black
notebook and say, "I'll just read two more."

It's a habit I don't understand. What if there's
a sigh of relief and the jangle of car keys? What
if someone shouts, "Over my dead body!"

It would be different if poetry were televised
like football. Then the two-poem warning might
make sense. People could stretch, open more chips,
or go to the bathroom.

There might be commercials for a rhyming
dictionary, sunsets in a can, or an 800 number
where you could talk to a drunken, abusive father
in case your own sweet and understanding parents
left you scrambling for subject matter.

Probably we just mean, "I know it's been a long
evening." It wasn't a good sign when the first reader
wheeled his epic in on a gurney. And that girl with
the bandaged hand who put down her chapbook
and sobbed left those of you in the already breezy
front row with wet feet.

But try not to think of pneumonia or the baby-sitter
or the freeway or even that person in tight pants
who came in alone.

Stick with me. You won't be sorry. I have saved
the best for last.

Nightclubs

I think I could sit forever at one
of those little tables just big enough
for a lamp, an ashtray, and two flutes
of champagne. The bar never closes,
the band never takes a break.

Time is not hurrying the corridors
of the world, but standing still
in the corner, smoking, listening
to the singer and whispering, "You
look beautiful tonight," pretending
to be human until that sad occupation

makes him turn away and retrieve
from the stunned hatcheck girl his
dark coat and shiny hourglass.

1989

Because AIDS was slaughtering people left and right,
    I went to a lot of memorial services that year.
There were so many, I'd pencil them in between
    a movie or a sale at Macy's. The other thing that
made them tolerable was the funny stories people
    got up and told about the deceased: the time he
hurled a mushroom fritata across a crowded room,
    those green huraches he refused to throw away,
the joke about the flight attendant and the banana
    that cracked him up every time.

But this funeral was for a blind friend of my wife's
    who'd merely died. And the interesting thing
about it was the guide dogs; with all the harness
    and the sniffing around, the vestibule of the church
looked like the starting line of the Iditarod. But
    nobody got up to talk. We just sat there,
and the pastor read the King James version. Then he
    said someday we would see Robert and he us.

Throughout the service, the dogs slumped beside their
    masters. But when the soloist stood and launched
into a screechy rendition of "Abide With Me," they sank
    into the carpet. A few put their paws over their ears.
Someone whispered to one of the blind guys; he told
    another, and the laughter started to spread. People
in the back looked around, startled and embarrassed,
    until they spotted all those chunky Labradors
flattened out like animals in a cartoon about
    steamrollers. Then they started, too.

That was more like it. That was what I was used to—
    a roomful of people laughing and crying, taking off
their sunglasses to blot their inconsolable eyes.